WORLD ELECTORAL PROCESSES

World Governments Series

•●●●●●●●●●●●●●●●●

Written by Darcy B. Frisina, M.Ed.

GRADES 5 - 8
Reading Levels 3 - 4

Classroom Complete Press

P.O. Box 19729
San Diego, CA 92159
Tel: 1-800-663-3609 / Fax: 1-800-663-3608
Email: service@classroomcompletepress.com

www.classroomcompletepress.com

ISBN-13: 978-55319-353-1
ISBN-10: 1-55319-353-9

© 2007

Critical Thinking Skills

World Electoral Processes

Skills For Critical Thinking	Systems and Reform							
	History of the Voting System	Legitimacy of Democratic Government	Presidential System	Parliamentary System	Dictatorship Government	Suffrage	Systems and Reform	Writing Tasks
LEVEL 1 Knowledge								
• List Details/Facts			✓	✓	✓	✓	✓	
• Recall Information	✓	✓	✓	✓	✓	✓	✓	✓
• Match Vocabulary to Definitions	✓		✓			✓		
• Recognize Validity (T/F)	✓					✓		
LEVEL 2 Comprehension								
• Summarize	✓	✓	✓					
• Describe	✓	✓		✓	✓		✓	
• Interpret			✓	✓	✓		✓	
• Compare/Contrast			✓	✓				✓
LEVEL 3 Application								
• Use Outside Research Tools		✓	✓	✓	✓	✓	✓	✓
• Application to Own Life	✓							
• Organize Facts	✓							
• Apply Vocabulary Words in Sentences		✓			✓		✓	
LEVEL 4 Analysis								
• Draw Conclusions					✓			
• Indentify Cause and Effect						✓	✓	
• Make Inferences					✓		✓	
LEVEL 5 Synthesis								
• Prediction		✓					✓	
• Imagine Self Interacting with Subject	✓	✓	✓					✓
• Create a Plan								✓
• Imagine Alternatives				✓		✓	✓	
LEVEL 6 Evaluation								
• State and Defend an Opinion	✓		✓	✓		✓	✓	✓
• Evaluate	✓				✓			✓

Based on Bloom's Taxonomy

Contents

FREE! 6 Bonus Activities!

3 EASY STEPS to receive your 6 Bonus Activities!
- Go to our website:
  www.classroomcompletepress.com\bonus
- Click on item CC5762 – World Electoral Processes
- Enter pass code CC5762D

Assessment Rubric

World Electoral Processes

Student's Name: _____ Assignment: _____ Level: _____

	Level 1	**Level 2**	**Level 3**	**Level 4**
Comprehension of Electoral Processes	Demonstrates a limited understanding of concepts. Requires teacher intervention.	Demonstrates a basic understanding of the concepts covered.	Demonstrates a good understanding of the concepts covered.	Demonstrates a thorough understanding of the concepts covered.
Response to the Text	Expresses responses to the text with limited effectiveness, inconsistently supported by proof from the text.	Expresses responses to the text with some effectiveness, supported with some proof from the text.	Expresses responses to the text with appropriate skills, supported with appropriate proof from the text.	Expresses thorough and complete responses to the text, supported by concise and effective proof from the text.
Analysis and Application of Key Concepts (i.e., evaluates a situation, relates and applies concepts to own context, conducts research, and collects relevant information)	Interprets and applies various concepts in the the text with few, unrelated details incorrect analysis.	Interprets and applies various concepts in the text with some detail, but with some inconsistent analysis.	Interprets and applies various concepts in the text with appropriate detail and analysis.	Effectively interprets and applies various concepts in the text with consistent, clear, and effective detail and analysis.

STRENGTHS:

WEAKNESSES:

NEXT STEPS:

Teacher Guide

Our resource has been created for ease of use by both TEACHERS and STUDENTS alike.

Introduction

This resource provides ready-to-use information and activities for remedial students in grades five to eight. Written to grade and using simplified language and vocabulary, **SOCIAL STUDIES** concepts are presented in a way that makes them more accessible to students and easier to understand. Comprised of reading passages, student activities and overhead transparencies, our resource can be used effectively for whole-class, small group and independent work.

How is Our Resource Organized?

STUDENT HANDOUTS

This resource has been created for ease of use by both teachers and students alike. **BEFORE YOU READ** questions (1 page) and **AFTER YOU READ** questions (2 pages) for each reading passage focus on the five themes of geography as key concepts to better understand the world in which we live. Bloom's taxonomy of thinking skills has been used in the development of the activities.

- The **BEFORE YOU READ** activities prepare students for reading by introducing the issues, concepts, and vocabulary to be found in the upcoming readings. They stimulate background knowledge, and guide students to make connections between what they already know and what they will learn. Important issues, concepts, and vocabulary are presented in short, easy-to-complete activities.

- The **AFTER YOU READ** questions check students' comprehension of the readings and extend their learning. Students are asked to give thoughtful consideration of the text through a variety of multiple-choice questions, creative and evaluative short-answer questions, and activities that extend and apply the students' learning through simple research activities and questions that ask them to apply the concepts to their own interests and circumstances.

The Assessment Rubric (*page 4*) is a useful tool for evaluating students' responses to many of the activities in our resource. The Comprehension Quiz (*page 48*) can be used for either a follow-up review or assessment at the completion of the unit.

PICTURE CUES

This resource contains three main types of pages, each with a different purpose and use. A **Picture Cue** at the top of each page shows, at a glance, what the page is for.

 Teacher Guide
- Information and tools for the teacher

 Student Handouts
- Reproducible worksheets and activities

 Easy Marking™ Answer Key
- Answers for student activities

EASY MARKING™ ANSWER KEY

Marking students' worksheets is fast and easy with this **Answer Key**. Answers are listed in columns – just line up the column with its corresponding worksheet, as shown, and see how every question matches up with its answer!

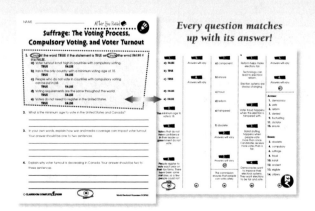

Every question matches up with its answer!

Bloom's Taxonomy

Our resource is an effective tool for any SOCIAL STUDIES PROGRAM.

Bloom's Taxonomy* for Reading Comprehension

The activities in our resource engage and build the full range of thinking skills that are essential for students' reading comprehension and understanding of important social studies concepts. Based on the six levels of thinking in Bloom's Taxonomy, and using language at a remedial level, information and questions are given that challenge students to not only recall what they have read, but move beyond this to understand the text and concepts through higher-order thinking. By using higher-order skills of application, analysis, synthesis and evaluation, students become active readers, drawing more meaning from the text, attaining a greater understanding of concepts, and applying and extending their learning in more sophisticated ways.

Our resource, therefore, is an effective tool for any Social Studies program. Whether it is used in whole or in part, or adapted to meet individual student needs, our resource provides teachers with essential information and questions to ask, inspiring students' interest, creativity, and promoting meaningful learning.

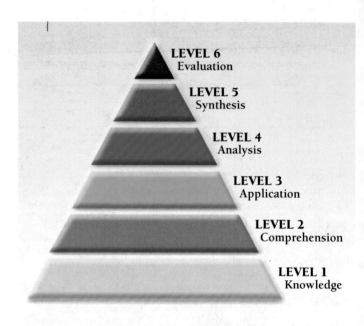

**BLOOM'S TAXONOMY:
6 LEVELS OF THINKING**

*Bloom's Taxonomy is a widely used tool by educators for classifying learning objectives, and is based on the work of Benjamin Bloom.

Vocabulary

ancient	dictator	install	representatives
bill	election	legislature	select
cabinet	eligible	medieval	suffrage
cast	enforce	military	tampered
citizens	ensure	monarch	term
colonization	execute	obsolete	veto
component	fluctuating	option	violate
compulsory	fraud	parliament	
democracy	funding	persecution	
denied	indefinite	reform	

History of the Voting System

1. **Match each of the words below with the correct meaning. You may use a dictionary to help you.**

a	option	_____	A	A government by the people
b	ancient	_____	B	From the Middle Ages
c	cast	_____	C	To choose by voting
d	election	_____	D	Very old
e	democratic	_____	E	To place a vote
f	medieval	_____	F	A choice

2. **Voting is an important part of being a citizen. List three reasons why it is important to vote.**

   a) _____

   b) _____

   c) _____

3. **There are several countries in the world where people are not allowed to vote. This could be because of their race, religion, or gender. Do you believe this is fair? Answer in two to three complete sentences.**

   _____

   _____

   _____

   _____

History of the Voting System

Voting is an important part of a democratic government. It is a way for the people to choose between a number of different options. Voting can be used in everyday life in order to make decisions. Voting is used in elections because it allows the people to select the leaders they believe in most.

Voting has been used by governments for thousands of years. It is believed that voting was first created by the ancient Greeks in the 6th century B.C. There are no exact records, but most experts believe voting starting around 508 B.C.

In ancient Greece, only male landowners could vote. This means that there were very few votes. These votes were written on broken pots and then counted. This way of voting was also used to choose leaders in ancient India, Pakistan, and Afghanistan.

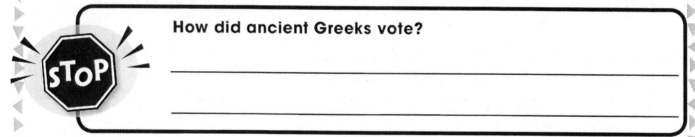

How did ancient Greeks vote?

_____

_____

In medieval Venice, a new form of voting was created in the 13th century. This new type of voting is called "approval voting". In this system, voters cast a vote for every choice they feel is acceptable. They do not vote for people they do not like.

Medieval Venetians elected representatives to the Great Council. This group had forty members. This was one of the models for the parliamentary system of government.

History of the Voting System

Voting requirements have changed quite a bit throughout history. Not every person has been allowed to vote. Many countries only allowed male land owners to vote. Other countries did not allow people who were not white to vote.

The United States was one of those countries. African-American citizens were not allowed to vote until 1860. There are still some countries in the world where not every citizen is allowed to vote because of their race or religion.

Around the world, women have not always been able to vote. Canada only allowed women to vote in three provinces in 1916. Other provinces followed in the next few years. In the United States, women got the right to vote in 1920.

Other countries have been slow to allow women to vote. Switzerland did not allow women to vote until the 1970's. Several countries in the Middle East still do not allow women to vote. Saudi Arabia is one of those countries.

There are a few international groups that work to protect voting rights around the world. They work to make sure that everyone who has the right to vote can vote freely. They also work to try to gain voting rights for all citizens so that all the people can vote, not just a few.

Two of these groups, the United Nations Fair Elections Commissions and the Carter Center, have been very active in helping elections in foreign countries remain safe.

Voting Line, Iraq

History of the Voting System

1. Circle if the word **TRUE** if the statement is TRUE **or** Circle the word **FALSE** if it is FALSE.

   a) Voting was created by the ancient Romans.

       TRUE   **FALSE**

   b) Voting allows the people to choose their leaders.

       TRUE   **FALSE**

   c) Switzerland was the first country to let women vote.

       TRUE   **FALSE**

   d) Every country allows all their citizens to vote.

       TRUE   **FALSE**

   e) Medieval Venetians elected members to the Great Council.

       TRUE   **FALSE**

   f) The Carter Center helps elections around the world.

       TRUE   **FALSE**

---

2. Circle the event that happened first.

   a)   Greeks voted using broken pieces of pots.
   Venetians used approval voting.

   b)   Women had the right to vote in Saudi Arabia.
   Women had the right to vote in Canada.

---

3. **The medieval Venetians created approval voting. In your own words, summarize how approval voting works. Your answer should be two to three sentences.**

   _____

   _____

   _____

   _____

History of the Voting System

4. Imagine you could interview a woman in Saudi Arabia who is not allowed to vote in her country's elections. List three questions you would ask her about this topic.

a) _____

b) _____

c) _____

5. If you were a leader in a country like Saudi Arabia that did not allow women to vote, would you change this? Your explanation should be at least two to three sentences.

_____

_____

_____

_____

_____

_____

_____

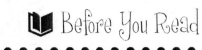

NAME: _____

The Legitimacy of Democratic Government

1. **Complete each sentence with a word from the list. Use a dictionary to help you.**

> violate   citizens   democracy
> representatives   persecution

a) The _____ are elected by the people.

b) If you _____ the rules, you will be grounded.

c) A _____ is a government for the people.

d) The people who live in an area or country are the _____.

e) Many people have left their own country because of _____.

2. **Using the resources in your classroom, list five countries that are democracies.**

a) _____

b) _____

c) _____

d) _____

e) _____

3. **Now use your classroom resources to list three countries that are not democracies.**

a) _____

b) _____

c) _____

The Legitimacy of Democratic Government

Democracy means rule of the people. It describes a government where the people who live in that country choose their representatives. These representatives are chosen in an election and represent the citizens when making decisions for the good of the community or country.

How are representatives chosen in a democracy?

_____

_____

_____

In a democracy, all citizens should be seen as equal by the government. This means that every citizen should have the right to vote, no matter their race, religion, or beliefs. Every citizen has the right to vote in a true democracy.

Ancient Greeks in Athens were the first to have a democracy. However, slaves and women were not able to vote. Since the majority of the people living in Athens were slaves or not citizens, very few people were allowed to vote. Democracy in ancient Greece did not last long for this reason.

Other ancient cultures had democratic governments, but not all of the people were allowed to vote. These ancient cultures include India, Rome, Pakistan, and the Iroquois tribe in North America. However, the Iroquois only allowed the oldest females of the family to elect and remove leaders.

The Legitimacy of Democratic Government

A democracy should also protect the human rights of all its citizens. This means that people can speak freely and express their opinions without fear of persecution. Democracies allow people to read and study whatever they want. They can also vote for whoever they want during elections.

If someone is arrested in a democracy, they will receive a fair trial. They will have an opportunity to present their case to the court and will receive a fair judgment. They will not be put in prison unfairly and without good reason.

Many countries in the world, including the United States, Canada, the United Kingdom, and India are democracies. They allow their citizens to elect their representatives, protect their freedoms, and protect their basic human rights.

Many other countries also claim to be democracies. However, they are not true democracies. One reason may be because they either do not allow all of their citizens to vote. Bhutan and Saudi Arabia do not allow all citizens to vote.

Another reason may be because they violate some of the idea of a true democracy. Some countries say they are democracies, but they do not allow people full freedom.

For example, they may not allow people to express their opinions without having to suffer a penalty. They also may not allow people to read certain books or study certain subjects.

For these reasons, international groups are working to help the people in these countries get basic human rights through democracy.

NAME: _____

The Legitimacy of Democratic Government

1. Below is a list of six ideas. (Circle) the four ideas that are democratic ideas.

Protects human rights

Allows only land owners to vote

Does not allow people to study other governments

All citizens can vote

Protects the freedoms of its citizens

People are allowed to express their opinions freely

2. The ancient Greeks were the first to have a democratic government. Explain how the democracy of ancient Greece is different from true democracies now. Your answer should be one to two complete sentences.

_____

_____

_____

3. Explain why democracy failed in ancient Greece. Your answer should be one to two sentences.

_____

_____

_____

4. Compare the Iroquois democracy to other democracies at that time. Tell how they are alike and different. Your answer should be three to four sentences.

_____

_____

_____

_____

The Legitimacy of Democratic Government

5. Democracy spread quickly in the 20th century. Predict how democracy will change in the 21st century. Your answer should be three to four complete sentences.

_____

_____

_____

_____

_____

_____

_____

6. Do you believe a democracy represents the people? State your opinion in three to four complete sentences.

_____

_____

_____

_____

_____

_____

_____

_____

 Before You Read

Presidential System of Government

1. **Write each word from the list next to the correct meaning. Use a dictionary to help you.**

term	bill	cabinet
legislature	veto	

a) A group of people that make laws _____.

b) The power of a president to stop a law _____.

c) The first draft of a law _____.

d) The president's group of advisors _____.

e) A period of time _____.

2. **Many governments follow the presidential system of government. List five countries that have presidents as their leaders. Use the resources in your classroom to help you.**

a) _____

b) _____

c) _____

d) _____

e) _____

3. **Being president can be a challenge. Imagine you are the president of your country. Identify three issues you would address if you were president.**

a) _____

b) _____

c) _____

Presidential System of Government

The presidential system of government is a government ruled by a president who won a national election. The president is both the head of state and the head of the government.

The president is elected by the people in a free election. Each government has a fixed presidential term of several years. The most common term is four years. During this time, the president acts as a representative of the people who elected him when meeting with foreign representatives and making important decisions.

In most governments that use the presidential system, the president cannot introduce bills to the legislature. However, there is one exception. In Puerto Rico, the president can introduce a bill. This does not usually occur in other countries that follow the presidential system of government.

The president also cannot vote in the legislature on bills or other issues. If the president does not agree with a bill passed by the legislature, the president can veto the bill. When the president vetoes a bill, the bill is sent back to the legislature to be approved or not approved. If the bill does not receive enough support from the legislature at this point, the bill dies. If the bill does get enough support, it becomes a law.

STOP

Why does a president veto a bill?

_____

_____

NAME: _____

Presidential System of Government

The presidential system of government does not allow one part of government to become more powerful than another. The president does not have complete power because he cannot make laws. The legislature does not have the power to carry out laws. Both parts of the government work separately to make the best decisions for their representatives.

The White House, Washington USA

Most presidents have a group of experts who give them advice. This group is called a cabinet. When making important decisions, the president usually gets the advice of the cabinet before making a final decision. The president does not have to follow the advice of his cabinet, but does consider the advice when making a decision.

Presidents also have a person who works directly with them. This person is called either the vice-president or the deputy president. The vice-president usually is selected by the president before the election. Some countries, however, elect their vice-president separately.

The vice-president takes over some of the ceremonial duties of the president if the president is too busy. The vice-president advises the president and is the next person in line to be president should the president die in office.

In the United States, another important job of the vice-president is to work with the Senate. If there is a tie in the Senate, the vice-president casts the vote that breaks the tie. The president cannot vote to break a tie.

Presidential System of Government

1. **What are the two job titles used to describe the job of president?**

   _____

   _____

2. **Below are five jobs. Circle the three jobs of the vice-president.**

   Attends ceremonial duties for the president

   Is the next in line should the president die

   Helps create laws

   Vetoes bills

   Advises the president

3. **The president of Puerto Rico has a power that is different from the traditional role of president in other countries. Explain this difference. Your answer should be one to two complete sentences.**

   _____

   _____

   _____

4. **Do you believe this difference is in the best interest of Puerto Rico? Express your opinion in two to three sentences.**

   _____

   _____

   _____

   _____

Presidential System of Government

5. The vice-president has the power to break a tie in the Senate. The president does not have this power. Do you think the president has influence on the vice-president's decision? Explain your answer in two to three sentences.

_____

_____

_____

_____

6. The president has to share powers with the legislature in the presidential system. Predict what would happen if the president has total power and did not share power. What do you think would happen to the country? Your answer should be four to five complete sentences.

_____

_____

_____

_____

_____

_____

_____

Parliamentary System of Government

1. **Complete each sentence with a word from the list. Use a dictionary to help you.**

execute	parliament	select
monarch	indefinite	

a) The beach is closed for an _____ period of time.

b) _____ passed a new safety law this week.

c) Only skilled riders can _____ skateboard tricks.

d) It is difficult to _____ one cake because they all look delicious.

e) The _____ waved to the crowd at the state parade.

2. **Many governments follow the parliamentary system of government. List five countries that follow the parliamentary system. Use the resources in your classroom to help you.**

a)_____

b)_____

c)_____

d)_____

e)_____

Parliamentary System of Government

The parliamentary system of government is a government where the ability to create and execute laws is held by the legislature. The legislature is often called a Parliament. This is the most common system of government in the world.

Countries with a parliamentary system of government do not elect their head of government. They elect their representatives in the Parliament. The members of Parliament then select the head of government. In other words, the people of the country do not decide who should be their prime minister.

Once the Parliament selects a head of government, the head of state must approve the choice. In many countries, the head of state is a monarch. In other countries, the head of state is a president. The head of state participates in ceremonies and agrees to the laws created by the representatives. They do not make laws.

There are several different names for the head of government. This depends on the country. In England, the head of government is called the prime minister. This is the most common name. In Italy, the head of the government is called the premier. In a few countries, the head of government is called a president.

Prime ministers select a cabinet just like a president in the presidential system of government. These advisors give advice to the prime minister and support the decisions made by the prime minister. The prime minister does not have to

What are the three different names used for the head of government around the world?

_____

_____

Parliamentary System of Government

follow the cabinet's advice, but they do listen to their suggestions when making decisions.

Prime ministers are chosen for an indefinite period of time. This means that the prime minister stays in power as long as the Parliament supports the prime minister. If Parliament no longer supports the prime minister, the prime minister and his cabinet are expected to step down.

Many people believe that the parliamentary system best represents all the people of a country. Members of a Parliament can represent different races, social groups, and religious groups more directly than in the presidential system.

This is because more people have more direct impact on the creation of laws and decisions than in the presidential system. Only the president has the executive power in the presidential system, but those powers are shared by a group of people in the parliamentary system.

Other people believe the parliamentary system is better because it is easier to pass laws than the presidential system. This is because the prime minister is selected by the Parliament. In the presidential system, laws that are necessary may not be approved if the president and representatives are from different political parties and do not agree.

Parliamentary System of Government

1. Below are six statements. (Circle) **the three statements that are true about the parliamentary system of government.**

The head of state approves the prime minister.

The prime minister creates the laws of a country.

Parliament is elected by the people.

Parliament chooses the prime minister.

The prime minister is elected by the people.

Only the prime minister has executive power.

2.   What is the role of the head of state?

_____

_____

_____

3.   In your own words, describe how a person becomes the prime minister. Your answer should be three to four sentences.

_____

_____

_____

_____

_____

NAME: _____

Parliamentary System of Government

4. Explain why it is easier to pass laws in the parliamentary system than in the presidential system. Your answer should be at least three to four sentences.

_____

_____

_____

_____

5. Do you think the people should elect their head of government or do you think the representatives elected by the people should choose their head of government? Your answer should be three to four sentences.

_____

_____

_____

_____

_____

NAME: _____

A Dictatorship Government

1. **Match each of the words below with the correct meaning. You may use a dictionary to help you.**

a	dictator	_____	A	To set up
b	military	_____	B	Giving money to
c	colonization	_____	C	The army
d	install	_____	D	A ruler with absolute power
e	funding	_____	E	Populating an area or country

2. **After World War II and during the Cold War, many countries in Latin America, Africa, and Asia became dictatorship governments. Provide two reasons why this might have happened.**

a) _____

b) _____

3. **Identify five countries that had dictatorship governments after World War II. You may use the resources in your classroom to help you.**

a) _____

b) _____

c) _____

d) _____

e) _____

A Dictatorship Government

A dictator is a ruler who has absolute power. A dictatorship government is ruled by a dictator. Dictatorship governments are usually the result of military rule after a war or a conflict. They usually rise to power in an emergency situation where the people are eager for a leader. Dictators are often military leaders who were active leaders during the war or conflict.

Adolph Hitler 1889-1945

Dictatorship governments have been around for centuries. The Roman Republic had a position called Roman dictator. In times of trouble, these Roman dictators were given absolute power so that they could bring back order. However, men serving in this position had certain rules and laws that they were expected to follow.

Dictatorship governments changed over time. Dictators were no longer expected to follow the rules and laws of a government. Instead, dictators started to take complete power over a country.

After the end of World War II, many countries in Latin America, Asia, and Africa had dictatorship governments. This is because these countries had wars that ended European colonization. After fighting for their freedom, the military often installs a dictator so that one small group controlled by the military has all the power.

Why does the military install a dictator?

_____

_____

A Dictatorship Government

The Cold War between the United States and the Soviet Union also played an important part in the large number of dictatorships after World War II. Both the United States and the Soviet Union wanted to spread their political beliefs throughout the world in order to get more power. They did this by funding several civil wars, especially in Africa. These were brutal wars that led to the rise of a dictator.

Other countries installed dictatorships in order to protect themselves from the threat of capitalism and communism. They wanted to maintain their culture and avoid becoming just like other countries. In order to preserve their culture, they turned to a dictatorship government so that they could keep their national identity. This happened a great deal in Latin America.

In a dictatorship, the people do not have a voice in the government. The people do not have a chance to vote for their head of government. The dictator chooses all of the people who serve in the government. Countries that have dictatorship governments do not hold elections for these reasons.

Most dictatorships do not last for long periods of time. Many times, the dictator dies. Once the dictator is dead, there is often no clear way to install another dictator. The people are no longer afraid of the dictator, and they take their government back. Other times, there is another civil war, and the people take control of their government.

There are several international groups that help these countries re-establish fair and open elections. This helps them maintain control of their government.

A Dictatorship Government

1. **Read the five statements below. Circle the three statements that are true.**

There were a large number of dictatorships after World War II.

Many dictators were former military leaders.

There are open and free elections in dictatorship governments.

Dictatorships allow the people to control their government.

The dictator chooses the people who serve the government.

2. **What was the purpose of the Roman dictator?**

_____

_____

3. **Explain in your own words why most dictators were military leaders. Your answer should be at least two to three sentences.**

_____

_____

_____

_____

4. **How has the role of a dictator changed over time? Your answer should be two to three complete sentences.**

_____

_____

_____

_____

NAME: _____

A Dictatorship Government

5. Suppose you lived in a country with a dictatorship government. Would you be satisfied with your government? Explain your answer in two to three sentences.

_____

_____

_____

_____

6. Imagine you were a member of the military in a country. You have decided to install a dictator. Evaluate this decision. Did you make the best choice? Explain your answer in four to five sentences.

_____

_____

_____

_____

_____

_____

_____

Suffrage: The Voting Process, Compulsory Voting, and Voter Turnout

1. **Write each word from the list next to the correct meaning. Use a dictionary to help you.**

suffrage	compulsory	fluctuating
denied	enforce	eligible

   a) Qualified _____.

   b) To carry out _____.

   c) The right to vote _____.

   d) Turned down _____.

   e) Changing _____.

   f) Under command _____.

2. **Every country has its own requirements for voters. Using the resources in your classroom, find two of the requirements for voters in your country. List those requirements below.**

   a) _____

   b) _____

3. **Many countries have compulsory voting. Identify three countries. You may use the resources in your classroom to help you.**

   a) _____

   b) _____

   c) _____

Suffrage: The Voting Process, Compulsory Voting, and Voter Turnout

Suffrage is a citizen's right to vote. In different countries throughout history, many groups have been denied suffrage. This could be because of religion, race, age, gender, or social class.

In order to vote, a citizen must meet the requirements of the country. Every country has different requirements for voting. Most countries, including Canada and the United States, require voters to be at least 18 years old. The minimum voting age throughout the world falls between 15 and 21 years old. Currently, Iran is the only country with a minimum voting age of 15.

In most countries with a democratic government, citizens have the right to decide if they are going to vote. In these countries, there are no laws that require citizens to vote. If they meet the voting requirements and are registered to vote, they are free to choose if they want to vote.

This is not the case in every country. Some countries have compulsory voting. In these countries, citizens are required by the law to vote. Other countries that have compulsory voting do not force citizens to vote, but the citizen must still come to a polling place during the election so that their name can be checked from a list.

There are laws in these countries to enforce compulsory voting. Every eligible citizen must register to vote. If people do not follow the law, they can be fined, made to complete community service hours, or even placed in jail. The consequence of breaking the law is different in each country.

Suffrage: The Voting Process, Compulsory Voting, and Voter Turnout

STOP

What are three possible consequences of breaking the law?

_____

_____

Voter turnout is very high in countries that have compulsory voting. Countries that do not have compulsory voting experience fluctuating voter turnout. One of the reasons that citizens fail to vote is that they do not register to vote. In some countries, fewer than 80% of all eligible voters register to vote.

War and media coverage can also impact voter turnout. If voters do not have confidence in their government and their leaders, they tend not to vote. Many countries are continually looking for ways to increase voter turnout, including the United States.

In many democracies, voters must register with the government in order to vote in an election. In some countries, citizens who are eligible to vote will have to fill out a form in order to register. This is the process in the United States.

Canada allows people to register to vote on their yearly income tax forms. This was intended to make the registration process easier, but it is making the process more difficult. Some people have been denied the right to vote due to mistakes. This has resulted in lowering voter turnout.

Suffrage: The Voting Process, Compulsory Voting, and Voter Turnout

1. Circle if the word **TRUE** if the statement is TRUE or Circle the word **FALSE** if it is FALSE.

   a) Voter turnout is not high in countries with compulsory voting.
       TRUE   **FALSE**

   b) Iran is the only country with a minimum voting age of 15.
       TRUE   **FALSE**

   c) People who do not vote in countries with compulsory voting can be put in jail.
       TRUE   **FALSE**

   d) Voting requirements are the same throughout the world.
       TRUE   **FALSE**

   e) Voters do not need to register in the United States.
       TRUE   **FALSE**

2. What is the minimum age to vote in the United States and Canada?

_____

_____

3. In your own words, explain how war and media coverage can impact voter turnout. Your answer should be one to two sentences.

_____

_____

_____

4. Explain why voter turnout is decreasing in Canada. Your answer should be two to three sentences.

_____

_____

_____

Suffrage: The Voting Process, Compulsory Voting, and Voter Turnout

5. Do you believe compulsory voting encourages people to vote or threatens them into voting? Explain your answer in two to three sentences.

_____

_____

_____

_____

6. Imagine you lived in a country with compulsory voting. Do you think you would be more or less positive about the election process? Describe how you would feel. Your answer should be three to four sentences.

_____

_____

_____

_____

_____

_____

_____

_____

NAME: _____

Electoral Systems and Reform

1.   Complete each sentence with a word from the list. Use a dictionary to help you.

reform	ensure	fraud
component	obsolete	tampered

a)   We could not finish putting the table together because we are missing one

_____.

b)   I want to _____ that everyone has a cupcake before I give you

two.

c)   He committed _____ when he lied about the check.

d)   If you do not _____ you find yourself in serious trouble.

e)   We did not purchase the aspirin because it looked like it had been

_____ with.

f)   After the invention of the automobile, the horse-drawn carriage became

_____.

2.   Election reforms are intended to make elections safer and more fair. Make a list of
two changes that would make elections safer and more fair.

a) _____

b) _____

3.   The United Nations helps ensure safe elections. Using the resources in your classroom,
find two more facts about the United Nations.

a) _____

b) _____

Electoral Systems and Reform

Electoral systems are always changing because the needs and wants of citizens are always changing. As time goes by, countries may find that some of their electoral practices are out of date and need reform. Other countries may decide to become democracies.

A free and fair election is a major component of all democracies. If people do not have the opportunity to elect their leaders, their country is not a democracy. Whenever a country changes from a dictatorship to a democracy, there are safety concerns for the citizens.

Many times, the people who worked for the former dictator try to prevent people from voting. There are several organizations, such as the United Nations Fair Elections Commission, that can help ensure that the people can vote safely.

What does the United Nations Fair Elections Commission do?

_____

_____

Technology can also lead to electoral reform. Old voting systems may not be as accurate as new voting systems. In many countries, paper ballots that the voters punch out are becoming obsolete because they can be difficult to read. Many voting districts in the United States are changing from voting booths to computerized voting because the results are faster.

Voter fraud is a common concern for voters. There have been many elections around the world that have been effected by fraud. Voter intimidation is one way fraud can effect an election. People have even threatened violence and made bomb threats in order to disrupt elections.

NAME: _____

Electoral Systems and Reform

Sometimes the actual votes are tampered with in order to change the election results. Ballot stuffing occurs when one person votes more than once, causing one candidate to appear to receive more votes.

Another practice is to break the election equipment, making it impossible for people to cast their vote. Or, people can tamper with voting machines so that the voting results will be in favor of one candidate, regardless of how voters actually voted.

Ballot Box

In many places, voters have claimed to be other people in order to vote more than once. This is becoming more difficult in most countries because voters have to show identification before they vote. However, there are countries where people do not have identification, and this type of voter fraud is easier.

Voting machines have even been tampered with in order to change the results of an election. This can be done many different ways, including tampering with the voting machine software. As computer software becomes more complex, it becomes harder to tamper with election results.

Election systems are always changing in order to best serve the voters. Reform is a necessary part of the electoral process because it is designed to make sure elections are fair. True democracies are always looking for better ways to improve their electoral systems.

Electoral Systems and Reform

1. **Below is a list of five statements. (Circle) the three statements that are true about electoral reform.**

    Ballot stuffing is a fair electoral process.

    Reform helps make elections fair.

    Technology can lead to election reform.

    Voting machines cannot be tampered with.

    Electoral systems are always changing.

2. **What is voter fraud?**

    _____

    _____

3. **In your own words, explain how ballot stuffing can impact an election. Your answer should be two to three complete sentences.**

    _____

    _____

    _____

4. **Why are democracies always working toward electoral reform? Your answer should be one to two complete sentences.**

    _____

    _____

    _____

Electoral Systems and Reform

5. Predict what would happen if it was discovered your president or prime minister tampered with the election. Your answer should be at least three to four sentences.

_____

_____

_____

_____

_____

6. In your opinion, what should be the consequences of tampering with an election?

_____

_____

_____

_____

_____

_____

_____

Writing Tasks

1. Imagine that you could be the next leader of your country. What issues would be important to your voters. Write a speech, describing what you would do if you were given the power to lead your country.

2. Is your country's government a dictatorship, or does it follow either the presidential or parliamentary system of government? Use specific examples from the text you have read to support your answer.

3. Which form of government do you think best represents the citizens? Provide three examples that substantiate your opinion.

4. Complete the "Dictator vs. Elected Leader" graphic organizer. In your essay, compare and contrast the two different types of leadership. Be sure to give examples from your reading and research in order to support your answer.

5. Voter turnout is becoming a very large problem in the electoral process. What can be done to improve voter turnout? Create a plan that would help improve voter turnout in your area. Suggest three ideas to improve voter turnout and describe how these ideas can become reality.

6. Select a prime minister, president, or dictator from the 20th century. Complete the "Biography Timeline" graphic organizer. Write a biography of this leader, including how the leader came into power and how their leadership was impacted by world events.

Hands-on Activities

1. **Basketball Review Game:** At the end of the unit, you can use this game to help you prepare students for a unit quiz or test. Affix a basketball hoop to a wall in your classroom. On the floor in front of the basket, adhere three lines to the floor using tape. Assign each of these lines a point value. The closest line to the basket should be one point, the middle line should be two points, and the farthest line should be three points. Students will be divided into two teams, and one player will be at the hoop at a time. When the player answers the question correctly, they will throw a soft ball at the hoop in order to get points. If they miss the hoop or do not answer the question correctly, they will not be awarded points.

   Before starting the activity, you will need to prepare three categories of questions: easy (1 point), medium (2 points), and challenging (3 points). You can even involve the students in writing the questions. The day before the basketball game, ask each student to write one of each type of question. You can then go through those questions and select the best questions for the game.

2. **Hold an Election:** Select a policy or rule that would be relevant to the running of your classroom. This could include how chores are divided or whether or not homework will be assigned on weekends for one month. Students will have to work together to decide when the election will be held, design a ballot for the election, create a voting system that allows for voting privacy and security, and decide how votes will be counted.

3. **Roleplay:** In the paliamentary system, the House of Representatives allows members to deliver 90 second statements about issues that are important to them. Allow students to select their own issues and speak as a member of Parliament for those 90 seconds. Each student should have the opportunity to roleplay, so you will need to set aside ample time. You may decide to act as the Speaker, the moderator of the statements, or you may decide to select a student to be the moderator. If you do decide to allow a student to be the Speaker, make sure that student can keep track of the time limitations before you begin the statements.

Dictator vs. Elected Leader
Graphic Organizer

Directions: In the two outer columns, list the characteristics of each type of leadership. In the inner column, list the characteristics that are similar.

DICTATOR	SIMILARITIES	ELECTED LEADER

Biography Timeline Graphic Organizer

Directions: Use the timeline below to organize your biography project. In the empty boxes, write major events in the order they happened in that leader's life on the right side. On the left side, write the date of the events.

NAME: _____

Crossword Puzzle!

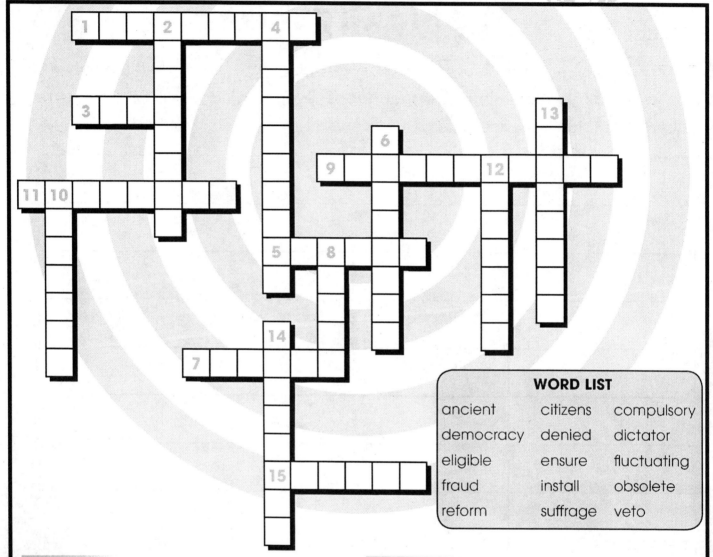

WORD LIST

ancient	citizens	compulsory
democracy	denied	dictator
eligible	ensure	fluctuating
fraud	install	obsolete
reform	suffrage	veto

Across

1. A government by the people
3. The power of a president to stop a law
5. To change
7. Turned down
9. Changing
11. A leader with absolute power
15. To make certain

Down

2. Out of date
4. Under command
6. The right to vote
8. Trickery
10. To set up
12. Very old
13. Qualified
14. The people of a country

NAME: _____

 After You Read

Word Search

Find all of the words in the Word Search. Words are written horizontally, vertically, diagonally, and some are even written backwards.

option	select	obsolete	bill
monarch	component	democracy	suffrage
fluctuating	election	install	veto
cast	dictator	fraud	denied
parliament	ensure	term	cabinet
reform	citizens	funding	enforce
medieval	military	execute	

T	C	E	L	E	S	R	S	E	T	U	C	E	X	E	G	H	F
U	W	E	O	L	T	K	O	B	S	O	L	E	T	E	N	J	L
F	Y	T	P	U	O	T	D	I	N	E	T	E	T	P	T	Z	U
H	O	P	T	I	O	N	O	I	T	C	E	L	E	N	A	C	C
M	T	E	S	U	F	F	R	A	G	E	N	T	R	F	M	U	T
Q	A	W	A	N	H	E	S	R	H	T	I	P	M	J	P	L	U
U	E	F	C	K	C	A	B	I	N	E	T	R	R	T	E	G	A
V	D	E	R	U	S	N	E	S	R	H	O	E	R	O	R	E	T
F	E	R	T	H	Y	V	S	E	K	T	W	F	O	Y	E	L	I
I	X	T	C	Y	F	L	L	U	A	B	J	O	T	U	D	E	N
N	W	E	O	A	S	A	U	T	T	O	J	R	K	F	J	E	G
S	E	F	A	M	V	N	C	D	V	H	I	M	A	D	Q	D	S
T	O	E	C	E	S	I	Q	A	C	E	R	C	U	V	A	C	X
A	S	W	I	C	D	E	U	R	V	O	M	A	T	K	P	O	O
L	T	D	T	J	K	D	A	C	R	Y	R	L	U	D	Z	M	A
L	E	N	I	A	B	N	S	H	U	F	C	T	W	E	N	P	P
M	E	R	Z	F	O	T	A	P	T	H	J	C	A	N	P	O	G
P	S	D	E	M	O	C	R	A	C	Y	R	E	N	I	T	N	L
O	I	R	N	E	Y	E	N	F	O	R	C	E	G	E	I	E	U
I	A	W	S	N	P	R	J	W	S	E	T	S	K	D	B	N	L
R	M	I	L	I	T	A	R	Y	G	S	I	Q	N	P	R	T	E
A	Q	L	U	T	K	E	T	A	K	H	R	U	O	L	U	T	J
P	A	R	L	I	A	M	E	N	T	P	F	L	R	B	I	L	L

World Electoral Processes CC5762

NAME: _____

Comprehension Quiz

Part A

25

Circle if the word **TRUE** if the statement is TRUE or Circle the word **FALSE** if it is FALSE.

5

a) The people elect the prime minister.

    TRUE   **FALSE**

b) Technology can lead to electoral reform.

    TRUE   **FALSE**

c) There are free and open elections in a dictatorship.

    TRUE   **FALSE**

d) The ancient Romans were the first to vote.

    TRUE   **FALSE**

e) Women have not always been allowed to vote

    TRUE   **FALSE**

Part B

Match the term on the left with the correct definition on the right.

 5

1 Term	**A**	The power to stop a law
2 Veto	**B**	To change
3 Democracy	**C**	A period of time
4 Compulsory	**D**	A government by the people
5 Reform	**E**	Under command

SUBTOTAL: /10

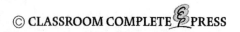

World Electoral Processes CC5762

Comprehension Quiz

Answer the questions in complete sentences.

1. Explain the purpose of the cabinet.

_____

_____

_____

(3)

2. Explain how technology can cause electoral reform.

_____

_____

_____

(3)

3. How long is a prime minister's term of office?

_____

_____

_____

(3)

4. Identify two reasons why people have been denied the right to vote.

_____

_____

_____

(3)

5. How does compulsory voting affect voter turnout?

_____

_____

_____

(3)

SUBTOTAL: /15

5. Answers will vary.

6. Answers will vary.

---

1. Protects human rights.

All citizens can vote.

Protects the freedoms of its citizens.

People are allowed to express their opinions freely.

2. Slaves and women were not allowed to vote.

3. The majority of people could not vote.

4. Answers will vary.

1.
a) representatives
b) violate
c) democracy
d) citizens
e) persecution

2. Answers will vary.

3. Answers will vary.
12

Representatives are elected by the people.
13

---

4. Answers will vary.

5. Answers will vary.

Votes were written on broken pots and counted.
8

1.
a) FALSE
b) TRUE
c) FALSE
d) FALSE
e) TRUE
f) TRUE

2.
a) Greeks voted using broken pots.
b) Women had the right to vote in Canada.

3. Voters cast a vote for every candidate they like. They do not vote for candidates they do not like.

1.
F
D
E
C
A
B

a
b
c
d
e
f

2. Answers will vary.

3. Answers will vary.

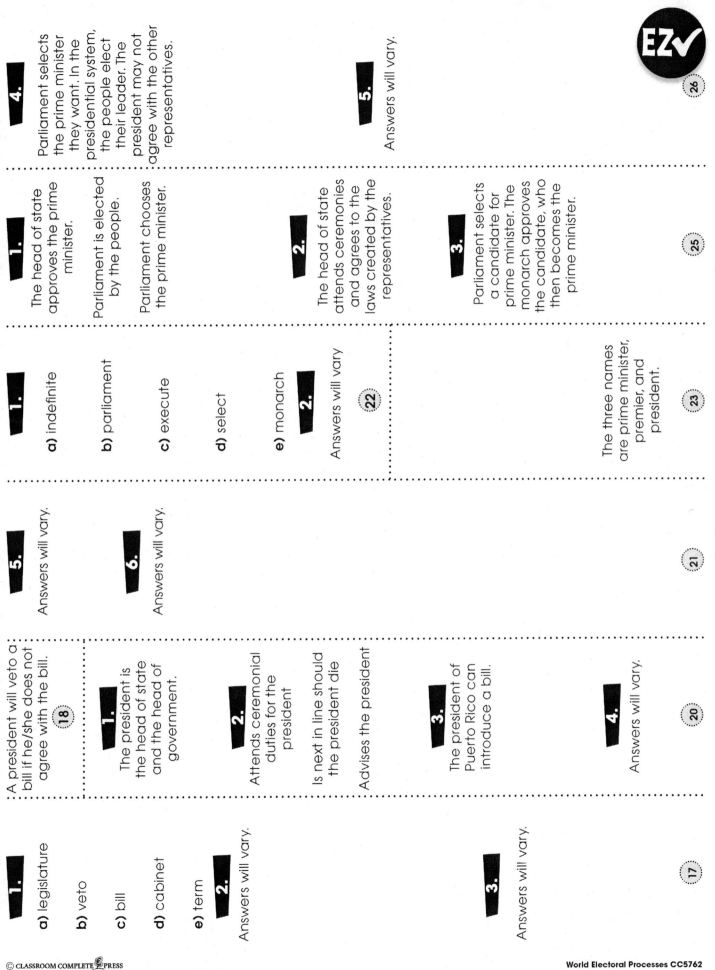

4. Parliament selects the prime minister they want. In the presidential system, the people elect their leader. The president may not agree with the other representatives.

5. Answers will vary.

1. The head of state approves the prime minister.

Parliament is elected by the people.

Parliament chooses the prime minister.

2. The head of state attends ceremonies and agrees to the laws created by the representatives.

3. Parliament selects a candidate for prime minister. The monarch approves the candidate, who then becomes the prime minister.

1.
a) indefinite
b) parliament
c) execute
d) select
e) monarch

2. Answers will vary

23. The three names are prime minister, premier, and president.

5. Answers will vary.

6. Answers will vary.

18. A president will veto a bill if he/she does not agree with the bill.

1. The president is the head of state and the head of government.

2. Attends ceremonial duties for the president

Is next in line should the president die

Advises the president

3. The president of Puerto Rico can introduce a bill.

4. Answers will vary.

1.
a) legislature
b) veto
c) bill
d) cabinet
e) term

2. Answers will vary.

3. Answers will vary.

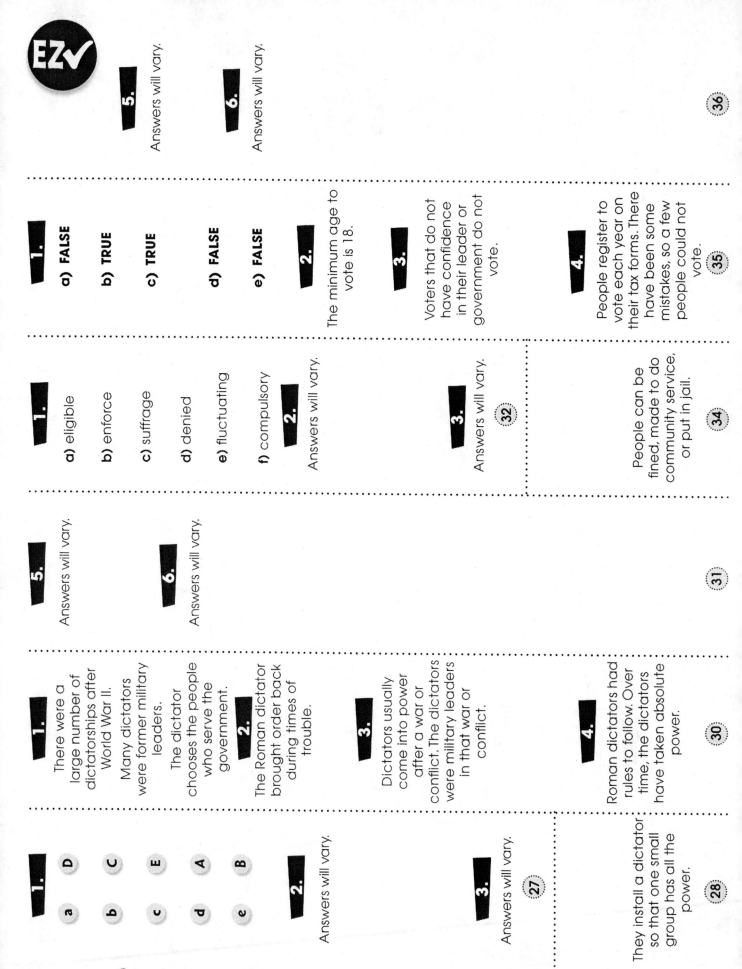

5. Answers will vary.

6. Answers will vary.

1.
a) FALSE
b) TRUE
c) TRUE
d) FALSE
e) FALSE

2. The minimum age to vote is 18.

3. Voters that do not have confidence in their leader or government do not vote.

4. People register to vote each year on their tax forms. There have been some mistakes, so a few people could not vote.

1.
a) eligible
b) enforce
c) suffrage
d) denied
e) fluctuating
f) compulsory

2. Answers will vary.

3. Answers will vary.

People can be fined, made to do community service, or put in jail.

5. Answers will vary.

6. Answers will vary.

1.
There were a large number of dictatorships after World War II.

Many dictators were former military leaders.

The dictator chooses the people who serve the government.

2. The Roman dictator brought order back during times of trouble.

3. Dictators usually come into power after a war or conflict. The dictators were military leaders in that war or conflict.

4. Roman dictators had rules to follow. Over time, the dictators have taken absolute power.

1.
D — a
C — b
E — c
A — d
B — e

2. Answers will vary.

3. Answers will vary.

They install a dictator so that one small group has all the power.

The crossword grid contains the following words: DEMOCRACY, VETO, DICTATOR, INSTALL, COMPULSORY, REFORM, SUFFRAGE, FLUCTUATING, ELIGIBLE, DENIED, CENSURE, ENSURE.

46

1.

a) component

b) ensure

c) fraud

d) reform

e) tampered

f) obsolete

2. Answers will vary.

3. Answers will vary.

37

The commission ensures that people can vote safely.

38

1.

Reform helps make elections fair.

Technology can lead to electoral reform.

Election systems are always changing.

2.

Voter fraud happens when the election is tampered with.

3.

Ballot stuffing happens when people vote more than once. Candidates receive more votes than is fair.

4.

Democracies want to improve their electoral systems. They want elections to be fair and safe.

40

5. Answers will vary.

6. Answers will vary.

41

Word Search Answers

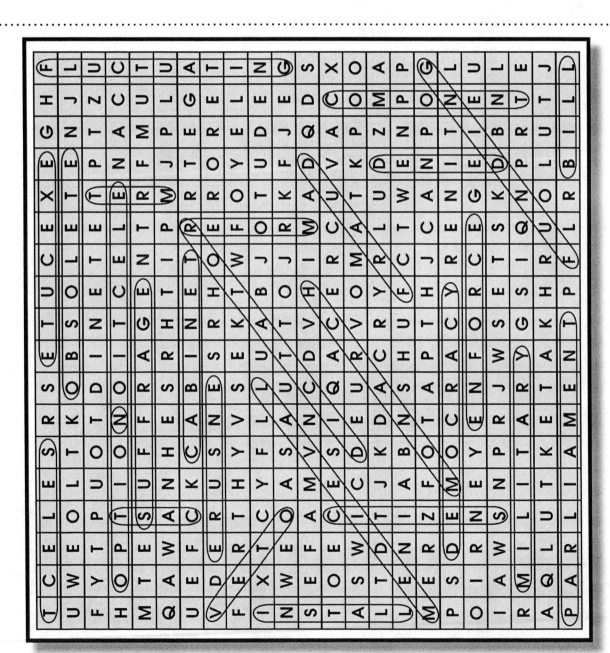

Part A

a) FALSE

b) TRUE

c) FALSE

d) FALSE

e) TRUE

Part B

1 C

2 A

3 D

4 E

5 B

Part C

1. The cabinet advises the leader.

2. Technology can make elections easier, faster, and more fair.

3. A prime minister's term lasts as long as they have Parliament's support.

4. Race, religion, gender, social status, and age are all reasons people have been denied the right to vote.

5. Voter turnout is higher in countries with compulsory voting.

The Parliamentary System of Government

The head of government is selected by Parliament. Parliament is elected by the people in free elections.

The head of government serves as long as they receive support from the legislature.

The Parliamentary System of Government

The head of government and the legislature share powers.

The head of government and head of state are two different people.

The Parliamentary System of Government

The Parliamentary System of Government

The head of government is selected by Parliament. Parliament is elected by the people in free elections.

The head of government and the legislature share powers.

The head of government serves as long as they receive support from the legislature.

The head of government and head of state are two different people.

Publication Listing

· · · · · · · · · · · · · · · ·

Ask Your Dealer About Our Complete Line

REGULAR EDUCATION

· ·

VISIT:

www.CLASSROOM COMPLETE PRESS.com

To view sample pages from each book

REMEDIAL EDUCATION

Reading Level 3-4 Grades 5-8

· · · · · · · · · · · ·

SCIENCE

ITEM #	TITLE
	ECOLOGY & THE ENVIRONMENT SERIES
CC4500	Ecosystems
CC4501	Classification & Adaptation
CC4502	Cells
CC4503	Ecology & The Environment Big Book
	MATTER & ENERGY SERIES
CC4504	Properties of Matter
CC4505	Atoms, Molecules & Elements
CC4506	Energy
CC4507	The Nature of Matter Big Book
	HUMAN BODY SERIES
CC4516	Cells, Skeletal & Muscular Systems
CC4517	Nervous, Senses & Respiratory Systems
CC4518	Circulatory, Digestive Excretory & Reproductive
CC4519	Human Body Big Book
	FORCE & MOTION SERIES
CC4508	Force
CC4509	Motion
CC4510	Simple Machines
CC4511	Force, Motion & Simple Machines Big Book
	SPACE & BEYOND SERIES
CC4512	Space - Solar Systems
CC4513	Space - Galaxies & The Universe
CC4514	Space - Travel & Technology
CC4515	Space Big Book

SOCIAL STUDIES

IEM #	TITLE
	MANAGING OUR WASTE SERIES
CC5764	Waste - At the Source
CC5765	Prevention, Recycling & Conservation
CC5766	Waste - The Global View
CC5767	Waste Management Big Book
	WORLD CONTINENTS SERIES
CC5750	North America
CC5751	South America
CC5768	The Americas Big Book
CC5752	Europe
CC5753	Africa
CC5754	Asia
CC5755	Australia
CC5756	Antarctica
	NORTH AMERICAN GOVERNMENT SERIES
CC5757	American Government
CC5758	Canadian Government
CC5759	Mexican Government
CC5760	Governments of North America Big Book
	WORLD GOVERNMENT SERIES
CC5761	World Political Leaders
CC5762	World Electoral Processes
CC5763	Capitalism versus Communism
CC5777	World Politics Big Book
	WORLD CONFLICT SERIES
CC5500	American Civil War
CC5501	World War I
CC5502	World War II
CC5503	World Wars I & II Big Book

LITERATURE KITS

ITEM #	TITLE
	GRADES 1-2
CC2100	Curious George (H. A. Rey)
CC2101	Paper Bag Princess (Robert N. Munsch)
CC2102	Stone Soup (Marcia Brown)
CC2103	The Very Hungry Caterpillar (Eric Carle)
CC2104	Where the Wild Things Are (Maurice Sendak)
	GRADES 3-4
CC2300	Babe: The Gallant Pig (Dick King-Smith)
CC2301	Because of Winn-Dixie (Kate DiCamillo)
CC2302	The Tale of Despereaux (Kate DiCamillo)
CC2303	James and the Giant Peach (Roald Dahl)
CC2304	Ramona Quimby, Age 8 (Beverly Cleary)
CC2305	The Mouse and the Motorcycle (Beverly Cleary)
	GRADES 5-6
CC2500	Black Beauty (Anna Sewell)
CC2501	Bridge to Terabithia (Katherine Paterson)
CC2502	Bud, Not Buddy (Christopher Paul Curtis)
CC2503	The Egypt Game (Zilpha Keatley Snyder)
CC2504	The Great Gilly Hopkins (Katherine Paterson)
CC2505	Holes (Louis Sachar)
CC2506	Number the Stars (Lois Lowry)
CC2507	The Sign of the Beaver (E.G. Speare)
CC2508	The Whipping Boy (Sid Fleischman)